CHANGELING

Clare Pollard was born in Bolton in 1978 and currently lives in East London. Her first collection of poetry, *The Heavy-Petting Zoo* (Bloodaxe Books, 1998) was written whilst she was still at school, and received an Eric Gregory Award. It was followed by *Bedtime* (2002), *Look, Clare! Look!* (2005) and *Changeling* (2011), all from Bloodaxe. *Changeling* is a Poetry Book Society Recommendation. Her first play *The Weather* (Faber, 2004) premièred at the Royal Court Theatre.

Clare supports herself by working as a broadcaster, teacher and editor. She has been Managing Editor of *The Idler* and is on the editorial board of *Magma*. She recently co-edited an anthology of emerging poets with James Byrne: *Voice Recognition: 21 Poets for the 21st Century* (Bloodaxe Books, 2009). She has written and presented two documentaries for television and one for radio, *My Male Muse* (2007), which was a Radio 4 Pick of the Year. She teaches for the City Lit and the Poetry School.

CLARE POLLARD
CHANGELING

BLOODAXE BOOKS

ISBN: 978 1 85224 911 3

First published 2011 by
Bloodaxe Books Ltd,
Highgreen,
Tarset,
Northumberland NE48 1RP.

Reprinted 2011

www.bloodaxebooks.com
For further information about Bloodaxe titles
please visit our website or write to
the above address for a catalogue.

Supported by
ARTS COUNCIL
ENGLAND

Cover design: Neil Astley & Pamela Robertson-Pearce.

Printed in Great Britain by
Bell & Bain Limited, Glasgow, Scotland.

For my mother,
who taught me to love rhyme
and 'The Wraggle Taggle Gypsies'

ACKNOWLEDGEMENTS

Acknowledgements are due to the editors of the following publications in which some of these poems first appeared: *Ambit, Book Club Boutique Newspaper, The Frogmore Papers, Identity Parade: new poets from Britain & Ireland* (Bloodaxe Books, 2010), *Interlitq, London Library Magazine, Magma, The Moth, Penpusher, The Poetry Archive, Poetry International, Poetry London, Poetry Review, Rising, Southword, The Wolf* and *Zafusy.*

'The Fairy Feller's Master-Stroke' was commissioned by the Tate. 'Broadstairs' started as a reworking of 'The Harrin's Heed', a folksong I heard at Broadstairs folk festival that begins: 'What'll wi dee wi' the harrin's heed? / We'll meck it inte loaves o' breed...' 'Reynardine' and 'The Two Ravens' are new versions of the traditional ballads 'Reynardine' and 'The Twa Corbies'.

Thanks are due to the Royal Literary Fund for granting me a fellowship whilst I was writing this collection. Thanks also to all those who read and gave helpful comments on these poems: the poets at The Lamb, Polly Clark, Antony Dunn, Julia Copus, Tim Turnbull, Hannah Sullivan, Melanie Challenger, and, most of all, Matthew Hollis.

CONTENTS

9 Tam Lin's Wife
10 The Panther
11 Pendle
12 The Confession of Alizon Device
14 Waiting for the Kettle to Boil, Lancashire
15 October Roses
16 First Sunflowers
17 Guide to the Birds of Britain and Europe
18 The Market
19 Adventures in Capitalism
20 'Can You Describe This?'
21 The Oil
22 Introducing that Most Marvellous Human Freak, the Bearded Lady Miss Lupin
24 The Fairy Feller's Master-Stroke
25 How to Recognise Saints by Their Attributes
26 Reynardine
28 Geraniums
29 Broadstairs
30 The Cruel Father
31 Spell
32 Guinevere
33 Empathy
34 Whitby
36 Dinner for Two
37 Revelations
38 An Island
39 Cassandra in Mycenae
42 Prescription
43 Lovely Trees
44 Thirtieth
45 The Whale's Tale
46 The Lure
48 Beads
49 Babylon
50 Amtssprache
51 The Language of Flowers *or* The Primrose

52   The City-dweller Laments
53   Lines Written on the Norfolk Broads
54   The Skulls of Dalston
56   Zennor
58   The Two Ravens
59   The Wood
62   The Caravan

Tam Lin's Wife

They sat us in a pale and private place,
quietly conveyed the worst –
explained the curse that was your fate
and how for one long, ill-starred night
you'd turn and burn, become all beasts
you could dream up.
I think that I cried out. They said
that if I want to have you
then I have to hold,
to hang on tight and not let go,
and not let go,
until you wake entire again within my arms –
pale skin, dark tufts of hair, long bones –
in crumpled daylight.
And now the sun has sunk, dark taken hold,
and in my hug you jolt
to sudden adder, X-marked, zigzagged, venom-
quick, then rear to brute-necked dog,
as black as forests and spume-jawed.
I tell myself that you are still my love
although I'm wet with blood, and you're a lynx
filthy with fingerprints, clean pink mouth snapping teeth
near heart, my throat.
I keep you caught and don't let go,
and don't let go,
and feel your skull become a bleach December sun,
your eyes hot coals, you burst to blaze: a wicker-man.
You're searing through my fingers,
molten lead.
Dear husband, all those things I prize in you –
your beauty, kindness, laugh –
are stripped off one by one
but even with them gone
my boy stares out from stricken shapes,
and love has no conditions. None.

The Panther

Frayed now, tongue-worn, the legend tells
that my parents – young and expecting me –
walked beneath blood-sprays of berries
plotting their future, when woods
convulsed with a pitiless roar;
thicket shook with the rage of an engine,
of dragons, of demons; of hunger made meat.
They ran all the way back to their bungalow.
A week later she heard the growl on radio:
If you hear this sound, beware.
It is a panther about to attack...

As a girl, I pored over theories:
big cats as escapees from menageries,
Victorian travelling circuses, prehistory, death...
I found a picture: *Melanistic Leopard*,
the eye like a chalk-pit or toad spawn,
teeth the sour colour of lambswool in the jaw.
And at dusk I sensed them out there; other –
the Beasts of Bolton, Bodmin, the Fen Tiger –
nuzzling a deer's bowels, careful as burglars.

In this city, now, I had forgotten them
in the scuffle of commonplace violence:
the friend beaten for a bike, his eye
popped out like a tiny moon; the needle-tracked
crackwhores smearing dung on our stair-well;
the lean dark men in hoods who may have guns.
But tonight, as I swallowed some small rejection,
I found myself willing it true:
longing caught in my throat for a panther's leap into view,
like the opposite of disappointment.

Pendle

When you must climb the hill, a woman's back bruised tender
with heather, & frozen puddles are fingernails gone bad,
then someone is to blame.

When you must wade for miles through ragged-robin, the rain-knives
& bog-rosemary to beg alms, when the neighbours owe you oats,
then someone is to blame.

When your children curdle like milk & turn one by one to clay dolls,
& your husband's fledgling-weak & you're a good Christian woman,
then someone is to blame.

When you dream of a woman fucking goats or men with horns;
of waking the witch, swimming her – lime-scalded & vice-tight,
then someone is to blame.

When you imagine her face yoked in a bridle & you want to slit
below her heart & suck there; weigh her weight against a bible,
then someone is to blame.

When the merlin steals hen-chicks & your fields are blighted
like a mouthful of black teeth, & your cow stark mad
then someone is to blame.

The Confession of Alizon Device
(a ballad)

When stumbling through sheep-coloured fog
    to the rough-lee, blood in my cough,
I slipped and fell into a ditch
    and saw hares laugh.

I cursed myself, began to cry,
    watched how the meadow-pipit's eyes,
inhuman, flickered over me.
    I felt despised.

The rain picked up into a storm,
    then out of weather, something foul:
the devil in a black dog's shape
    asked for my soul.

He said he'd help me to endure,
    so I let him lift up my skirts.
I let him suck upon my breasts,
    fuck me in dirt,

and I lay like a stone in mud,
    a wheatear dandled by a puss,
a bone pulled white by a wolf's jaw,
    I made no fuss.

Later a pedlar selling pins,
    sneered at these soiled and muddled rags,
'What would you have me do to him?'
    the black dog asked,

and I asked him: 'What can you do?'
    and he said: 'I can make him lame.'
'Then lame the pedlar,' I replied,
    and it was done.

And you ask me, do I feel shame?
    Well no, sir, that's what creatures do.
It was the moment of my life
    to hurt things too.

Waiting for the Kettle to Boil, Lancashire

Now I'm free of you I'm free to love you –
the nettles and the pissabeds
the arranwebs,

the rabbit-slavver of blackberries
buried in tetchy bushes,

your ale-coloured hills,
your short-crust pies.

I was the changeling daughter
you never understood –
spurning your lip and lads
for libraries and la-di-dah,

misreading your kind rains
as metaphor for my sad,
mithering heart.

Well, I'm no longer afeart –

I've tales to tell and am brimming with love
for what brought me to love, and here,
and here you are, still,
proud and proper mard –

your cratchy, flecky beauty,
your big tea-dark sky,

saying: *eee, love, now you're back,
d'you want a brew?*

October Roses

Roses this October
burnt red like plague posies –
rash for the world's fever,
a curse on our houses.

But then you were born in
the season's strange mildness.
My heart rose as you rose
in my arms, small witness.

With your nails as tiny
as droplets of spittle,
and your fragile mouth that
is like a dropped petal.

In far away lands there
are poor babies crying,
with milk-coloured eyes that
the black flies are circling,

and tree-tops are falling,
the birds falling with them.
The season is bleak but
new life can still blossom.

The October roses
burn, burn in the darkness.
Beautiful despite, no,
because of their lateness.

First Sunflowers

I watch them as they lean against the wall,
like lads behind a bike-shed for a smoke.
They nod, all skinny legs and awkward-tall;
the leaves shrug in the breeze. Their faces glow.
And things rush back: a boy who taught me lust –
my arid mouth, the sun behind, he leaned,
his hair a halo caught and drenched with light –
his sprouting tongue – his limbs – his teeth's warm seeds.

You see the way the florets are laid out?
This is the golden ratio. They catch
each other at the golden angle, meet
as when our youth and fire and ache all match.
Perfection's lost to me, but still the boys
are beautiful, and laughing as they blaze.

Guide to the Birds of Britain and Europe

The Wren is cunning. Soul of the Oak, the Druid-bird.
He trills: *steal my eggs and there'll be lightning.*

The Crow is known as Badb Catha, the Phantom Queen
who tends to warriors, gland and liver. She is the Terror.

The Swan hisses, hisses. Even her neck is a twisted *S*.
She's resident, common, depressed. She was once a princess.

The Nightingale has a buff eye-ring, she's tiny and brown
to hide from Tereus the hawk, who cuts out tongues.

And the white-headed, silver-cloaked Heron by the canal
is a wizard scrying in glass – there's a fish he cannot catch

but she's something else. Because of this, he loves her.

The Market

Is there anything sadder than London in winter?
The sky checks its queasy glow in glass towers.
At Brick Lane a man on a sheet
sells stolen bicycle seats,
a well-fingered copy of *Heat*, a doll's head,

and there's always some dude with three cups.
He says: *keep your eye on the cup with the money*,
but of course, the money is not in the cup.
There was never any money,
or the money was always in his hand.

Adventures in Capitalism

Nothing is real and I want it to stop.
I cut my wrists, but the blood looks like make up.

I slump in toilets snorting cocaine
but it doesn't seem true, just a grimy dream.

I wanted to *feel*, so had a tattoo done.
I chose a sea-blue anchor near the bone,

then saw it in a tabloid and felt a fake.
Crashed the car dad bought me. Nothing broke.

I went to see *Othello* swallow a lie
and cried at the end, but it was only a play.

Read some Rimbaud, bought a black polo-neck
and a bottle of absinthe, but felt like a prick.

I whisper: 'I love you' and 'Tie me down,'
but all that moan and fisting is just porn.

Signed an online petition but it made no difference.
I bought a house, but it's like playing house.

I own *How to Be a Domestic Goddess*,
but I've never cooked from it if I'm honest,

and the brownies and aprons are only props,
and my wardrobe's a Fancy Dress box,

and I yell at everyone who cares. I hurt them
because I need something to fucking happen.

'Can You Describe This?'

Take this down. Your future is a clutch of wonky ruins –
tigers prowl through high grasses in Tiananmen Square,
the Eiffel Tower's scar-coloured now, clotted with nests,
and speckled deer falter down Fifth Avenue. Every dam's
fallen to silt and spilt – dolphins swish past chandeliers –
and farmland, loosed from man's shoulder, is feral
with plumed thistle, mustard, lupine, flowering rape.
Guano plasters the Sistine Chapel. Libraries burn.

You imagine this beautiful, I know. Nearly want it.
But beauty's gone: wolves sniff Rodin's *The Kiss*,
gnaw it and leave. Love was your own disease,
and died, as head-lice died, along with you.
This is not justice. Lone and level sands don't mock.
There is only the boundless indifference you failed to see
when you were here to see, recording angels.

The Oil

is all stealth at first, hushed and lovely, a soft shifting shape in the deep; an expensive silk scarf loosed from a throat, groomed hair, ink scrawling an autograph, signing a pre-nup. In the aquamarine the plush gush has a caviar gleam, the colour of sultry night when we sprawl on our decks near Cannes or Mustique, hear liquidity lapping the hulls of our yachts. But then, it is suddenly not – it's morning and noticed and cameras are focused, and now the leak's writhing like shoals of suffering fish; like death in gulls' guts or bad debt. It's the spill of the ash from the second tower; a disgorging Helmand bomb; smoke's pour through the Underground. And we say *concern... heartbroken... keenly aware...* and besides, we've the cure – we have solvent, explosives, concrete, a saw. But we know, don't we? We know it's not true – we know that we can't put it back. What mortal could catch such a god – such omnipotent, muscular black? And see, see: how the slick spreads quick as denial or deforestation or AIDS or Al-Qaeda; as blood from the weapons expert's wrist; as blood's foul race across Neda's face in that YouTube clip

Introducing That Most Marvellous Human Freak, the Bearded Lady Miss Lupin

So here you are, sir,
in the shadow of the tilt,
the tented dark,

done with the stick and rag show:
the dizzying plinky-plonk galloper tunes,
the popcorn, piranhas & pin-heads,

the Half-Woman – a bust on her pedestal –
the mule-face who brays in his booth,
the Aethiop savage girl white as your wife,

and here I am,
wonder of wonders!
You look nervous, sir.

Is it the mewl of the tyger?
He's harmless, toothless.
The Bird-headed lady only squawks

for the Skeleton Man –
whose heart at last ate of itself –
& the grind shows are shutting,

the last thieves shushing
those foolish enough to be out.
So come on, closer:

trace the fur of my face,
moist at the mouth, pink lips,
the string-of-pearls teeth –

it's softer than sawdust,
softer than wolves,
a tangle to tug.

You will yearn to be butterfly-netted,
clamber its rope, part it
& sink in to drink,

& there's no whalebone stay
beneath this dress
to make me shit blood like your missus,

no, sir, just pelt:
its beast wagon scent,
a thick coat that needs tonguing clean.

I have watched many times
how desire contorts men –
how they tattoo my name down their spines,

how they flail on their nail-beds,
gulp fire, swallow swords;
how they make those sounds that are not words.

How I'll make the suit and snuff,
the ledgers and the way you pass the port –
all your life – feel like a ghost walk.

Some say we are clairvoyant,
saints or witches.
I say we make you want what you most fear –

if he is she, if wrong feels right,
then what are you, sir?
My fellow freak, come kiss this beard. Here.

The Fairy Feller's Master-Stroke
for Richard Dadd 1817–1886

As Queen Mab's mad to fly,
the axe must spilt
the hazelnut –
loose the brain of its meat,

make the hollow shell a wagon
with butterfly-wing upholstery,
her gilded fly itching at the reins.

You know she'll burrow
into skulls of dreaming men;
make them ache for shadows?

Of course you do.
And the earth alone is too much.
In Bedlam, i'th cage, there's still too much –
the Crazy Janes, their shit and squalls,
and just this patch of grass
you've watched nine years now –
nettle-daisy crowned, God's Spy.

You see the faerie-folk process,
genie-faced and gypsy:
the dandies, tatterdemalions, junketeers,
fay woodsmen, wenches,
tinker, tailor, leering satyr.
With their hubble-bubble pipes,
torn uniforms, queer stares,
this teeming life amongst the grubs
advances in its trance, your trance...

Poor fool.
In your prison you'll wear out
the packs and sects of great ones,
but never find a spell that undoes you.

What wounded flower did this?
What potion did they put upon your eyes?

24

How to Recognise Saints by their Attributes

Frideswide (Abbess) is rowed down the Thames by an angel.

Brigid (Virgin) has an onion in her hand.

Bridget of Kildare drips wax onto her arm.

Gertrude is known by a lily or mouse.

Froilanus (Bishop) lets a wolf carry his bags.

Peter of Verona has an axe in his head.

Polycarp (Martyr) refuses to adore an idol and/or is roasted in an oven.

Juthwara holds a soft, round cheese.

Lucy (Virgin, Martyr) holds her eyes in a dish.

Dominic is shown with a rosary. The devil, or a monkey, puts out his candle.

Reynardine
(a ballad)

A basketful of dappled eggs,
    was swaying on my arm,
the sky had darkened to a bog.
    Faint lights picked out our farm.

I'd pinched my cheeks to cloudberries,
    I'd bitten lips to haws,
for disappointing market lads
    who were not worth a pause,

but now in shadow cast by tor,
    I saw him slouching there –
that bold man with his feral smile
    and all that red red hair,

I said 'Kind sir, I ask of you
    please let a poor girl pass,
for I'm alone on this dark mount.'
    The man just blocked my path.

'Dear child,' he said 'I'd never harm
    so much as a pale lamb,'
and I turned pale and fainted, fell
    to arms safe as a den.

Swooning, I felt him muzzle soft,
    then pounce upon my face.
His mouth tasted of meat and moths,
    I writhed in his embrace.

Then pain – his teeth were meat-hook sharp,
    they butchered belly, throat.
He stripped my fingerbones of flesh.
    I screamed. He licked his snout.

And when I managed to come round –
    my innards in his paws –
I begged him weakly: 'What's your name?'
    He laughed. 'I won't be yours –'

'Though you might hunt forevermore,
    through fen, bone-cave or mount.
I live in a dark castle where
    there's everything you want.'

He said his name was Reynardine.
    I'm old with days I've roamed,
but the mountainside is barren,
    and I never get home.

Geraniums

The thing I fear most is diminishment.
Last night I was greedy for what could still be:
I want go to Rio, I slurred.
I wanna keep chickens! Try mescaline!

But tender mornings are about small things:
light tortoise-shelling the flat, a sip of juice, a DVD.
I've a fat stack of weekend papers
and my husband is whistling Spanish Flea.

On the windowsill, geraniums pulse,
sunsets on stalks, grenadine and coral.
I failed to water them. Fallen petals
are saying: *you must love this.*

Broadstairs

What'll I do with mackerel meat?
Make of it a damp pink beach.
What'll I do with codling eye?
Make of it a wet white sky.
What'll I do with pollock scales?
Make them into bright grey waves.

But what'll I do with the Hooden horse,
his sackcloth height, his snapping face,
his knees bound up with silver bells
that smash like sea on cockle shells,
as all the singers sing?

Of all the creatures by the sea,
this beast will make a dance of me,
The Wrotham Arms to The White Swan,
The Dolphin to The Albion.

What'll I do with spuming ale?
Make up pools that fizz and fill.
What'll I do with racing hours?
Make of them a Perseid shower.
What'll I do with world like this?
Make of it a lovers' kiss.

But what'll I do with the Hooden horse,
his knowing eye, his narrow nose,
his dark hunched shape that takes my breath
like whispered words beneath a cliff
as all the singers sing?

By snapping, smashing, spuming sea,
this beast will make a song of me,
The Wrotham Arms to The White Swan,
The Dolphin to The Albion.

The Cruel Father
(i.m. Rand Abdel-Qader)

In a land far from here,
a girl fell in love
with a man that she could never wed,

so her father choked her throat with his feet.
He stamped up and down.
He stabbed her small breasts with a knife.

He tossed her shrouded corpse
in a makeshift pit,
and spat on it.

And she was gone to him,
and this might have been an end,
but a white rose tree grew from the bones –

and a song-thrush landed on it
and the bird sang loud and clear:
'farewell, my love so dear.'

It trilled to all the world
as plainly as could be:
'There is my father who killed me.'

The police were men enough
to know what honour was.
They heard the song and slapped the father's back.

His sons said 'well done',
crushed the bloom, wrung the bird's neck.
They lit him up a cigarette.

Spell

Dying
is a magic word,
the most powerful spell.

A man utters it
and your living room
is Hell.

A man utters it
and your back garden
is Eden.

Apples are red hearts.
You long
to eat one.

Guinevere

None of the books said
you could love more than one man.
One king, one god, one only love:
those were the rules.
She loved her king, clasped
his warm hand at the joust,
drank wine and kissed
his laughing mouth.

But the knight was full of sorrow,
rode through weeping forests,
found her comb
and pulled out hairs between the teeth,
and put them fully to his eyes and mouth
a thousand times –
thought them brighter
than Midsummer.

He tried to hang himself,
cut fingers to the bone
to reach her room.
He was the best knight that there was;
how could she not ache
to hold him naked, break his awful fast,
to hold him fast to life,
sully her mouth?

Last night, in her, he took his earthly joy.
The court of Camelot play dice;
above the falcons wheel.
Her sheets are found
flecked with his blood.
She loves more than one man
and they will say this is not love at all,
although it feels like love.

Empathy

Do you want to feel how it feels?
Do you want to know that it doesn't hurt me?

KATE BUSH, 'Running up that Hill'

Hounds heave over the brow,
fast as the west wind, panting hunger,
as I run, stumble, *help me, please* –
can't you hear the fox's heart fit in my chest?

Wait – for you to care you need back-story.
Okay, let's start again:
imagine me at ten, gangly and grave.
I'm with a friend, trudging to her farm
through fields where wool is snagged on fizzing wires.

Now our girls' shrieks –
the sharp brown hounds,
how they worried me down, leapt and locked
to my thigh-meat;
the rain and the electrical fire of their teeth.

The owner howled: 'They're PLAYING'
as she loosed my leg from jaw.
Then sobbing came:
'Report them and they'll be put down – I'll be left so alone!'
Her tears blurred my eyes. I promised lies
to my parents about mouth-shaped stones

and, for weeks, traced the edge of that snag –
wondered, was tetanus bounding through my blood
or hunkered, other, in my heart?
In dreams they ate my friends and tore the lambs apart.

So when you read: TOT MAULED IN DOG HORROR
ask was I Kind or Irresponsible?
Did I show Forgiveness? Arrogance?
Was my sacrifice Self-Love?

I have never solved the problem of Empathy.
That old hag never spared a thought for me.

Whitby

You think to baffle me, you with your pale faces all in a row,
like sheep in a butcher's. You shall be sorry yet, each one of you!
You think you have left me without a place to rest, but I have more.

BRAM STOKER, *Dracula.*

Whirlpools of gulls whip over harbour –
clouds of yellow eyes –
and the stone sea's fearsome, melted
and roused to terrible passion.

Adders slip through moors.
On the promenade lovers
masticate winkles.
Punch kills the baby.

The roses on the fortune teller's
tatty hut are leeched,
and I've never bought a reading
for fear she'd shrug

for I am good and pure, a bore,
and in my room, again,
writing this diary, its prim script:
today piano, teas, I walked.

I took in air.
I made small talk.
My engagement ring tightens;
a noose on the gallows.

Yet something dark veins me,
as jet veins these cliffs –
black crystals brought
to toughness by time's weight.

When the tourists see
the mourning jewellery,
I've watched their covetous eyes;
how they gleam. And a fire

catches in me –
I'm the lighthouse lamp,
guiding something in –
the bay's sand fingers strain –

and a prow pierces the beach –
and a dark beast slumps up steps,
to the graveyard,
to the through-stones flat as beds,

the shuddering clouds,
the white moon like a fingertip
pressed up to glass –
a brute bat's wings are beating at the glass!

Come on then – I invite you in.
Why fight my own thought?
I'd roam this world too.
Penetrate it.

Feed on me that I can feed,
for I am sick of being tame.
Evil and freedom
are the same.

Dinner for Two

The CCTV's globed eye stares me down
as in the supermarket's blinding maze
I pick spice from the Indies, Asian prawns,
and blueberries as dark as Incan skies,
New Zealand lamb and Guatemalan peas.
A girl tuts: 'No – the airmiles –' at mange tout,
and I too feel that bland guilt nag at me,
but words of worlds are nothing next to you.

I take my plunder home, prepare a feast
to show I care, to counter your day's stress.
I pour Sancerre, like perfume on your feet –
the spoils of sea and sky; the East, the West.
The Earth contracts. Our room is everywhere.
In love one kiss, and any trade seems fair.

Revelations

And now, if there are any faults they are the mistakes of men
JOSEPH SMITH, Introduction to The Book of Mormon

God spoke to me
and he said tell my children to avoid prawns or condoms,
behead homosexuals, whip women who like trousers,
and 'I love Utah'.
He said 'I'd like you to issue a fatwa on Polio vaccines'.
Word was that you should give me all your life savings
as I'm his one prophet – to doubt is to sin –
and I've just remembered, yesterday, after dinner, God said:
'The dawn doth come when we must slaughtereth our enemies',
and obviously that's his words. I don't say 'doth'.
Also, we must create His Kingdom in Jerusalem,
and its yes on Iraq.
You want proof? Hear the miraculous truth!
God's angel led me to this book, right, that was made entirely out
          of Gold,
and I managed to translate it with a magic stone –
alas, the angel told me I could show the stone to no man,
and I lost the book, but still.
The Saved will laugh for all time when you end up in Hell,
with the grinding and the burning-oil thing
and the chamber of torso-severing –
seriously, I saw the pictures in the Book of Gold.
Yes, the one I lost.
God says that in order his work might go forward,
you should kill my ex-wife.

An Island

Circe's certain
in her hurt. Her pain's
her proof: it tipped
her isle askew.
Each conch
contains a howl.
Vengeance, she knows
will set the slant
world straight.
Men wade to shore
and Circe's sure
they're the same men

or close enough, rough
hands, straight hips,
the type who talk
of sharks and ships.
Circe's certain
in her pain; turns men
to lions, wolves or pigs.
They kill the deer,
and sleep in mud
and Circe sneers
(she knew they would.)
But still the shells
howl in themselves

and night brings storms;
the listing beach,
the tilting thought
the beasts aren't beasts,
but have her eyes
so sure with hurt
hate takes a shape
that looks like hers:
round hips, a witch's
mouth, thin arms.
It does not end,
this lurching harm.

Cassandra in Mycenae

So Agamemnon tugs a spluttering flap
in his daughter's throat,
and home is a trap.

In malignant Greek sun the Scops owl hoots,
and a wife will axe
at her husband's guts,

slop a slick maze in dust, children plot, things fall,
squalls of blood
flood the land...

And you don't believe me, of course –
the alternative's worse.
So go on, cover your ears –

you know what? I'm glad you don't hear.
It's gobbledegook, I'm a freak,
I lie I say this is only the start,

that emperors will make death sport,
people cast the first stone,
men invent thumbscrews, the Rack,

a chair you can dunk women in,
'Honour' killings and Pogroms,
Original Sin.

You find this depressing?
Dismiss me,
but the future will happen the same:

an Iroquois babe boil
with bubbling smallpox,
a whip flay a back to a sugarcane field,

a signwriter scribe: *Arbeit macht frei*,
faces melt in Japan,
child soldiers carry Kalashnikovs, coke-cans.

O every night Eric and Dylan
enter the school cafeteria –
towers fall – hysteria –

Yo lo vi. Yo esto también.
The Long March crawls
through my nightsweats, my mares,

then the Berlin Wall,
the gulags where men chew a maggot-laced horse,
lynchings, napalm, the S21,

Zodiac, Dahmer, the Wests,
the atomic bomb –
icebergs slouch into the sea...

The Snake licked my ears
and they spat in my mouth
when they gave me this curse,

and the earth is cursed,
so you're right to naysay.
Go on, raise an eyebrow, shrug it away –

buy raspberries in March,
the villa in Pompeii.
In my head it's rolling news,

and after a while being perfectly useless,
your face has to dry.
Your heart goes onto standby.

For all stories end with death,
those that don't are the teller looking away,
and I don't get that luxury.

See, now evening's come:
turtles cover their eggs on the beach,
mountain-top beacons burn.

The amethyst tapestry's spread on the floor,
Agamemnon's hand's on the door –
don't watch! Don't listen!

Darkness is sweeter than vision.
Bury your face in a rose, pour some wine, feel the in
and the out of your breath.

Ignore me, please. Ignore me and Death.

Prescription

I'm recommending Heartsease to still
the tear that rolls,
the brain that churns,
the springing cry in the chest that waits
as if in ambush.
If the Furies have your scent
you must need mercy –
that strain of mercy that Athena metes out
with her scales, her grey eyes.
Even Helen stirred Heartsease in her wine
with a grimy finger,
when she saw the damage done:
how hell had dawned within her arms.
Her wan face regained its charm.
Look how it comes, clean,
a blister-pack of swan's eggs;
new moons.
You should take it.
Take it.

Lovely Trees

That first autumn our home was ugly with dust;
infuriating with boxes, planks,
buckets we used to flush the loo.
We had no curtains.

Bed-level, you couldn't see the building site.
We'd wake to a square of tree against sky –
leaves yellow as *Pasteis de Nata*;
dawn-lit paper lanterns.

On one branch, a plastic-bag breathed.
On another, pigeons, still trying to nap,
kept themselves tucked in – plump grey jugs.

And below, of course, roots were gagging the drains,
graffiti-ing lightning on walls,
teasing cracks for rats,

and we knew, come New Year, the trees had to be felled –
just as we had to plaster, scrub, paint,
rewire, maintain, move on...

But still, each day you'd wake up
to those glowing tatters and smile.
Say: *the tree looks lovelier every day*.
And I'd nod, and push thoughts of winter away,
as all lovers must refuse the thought of winter.

Thirtieth

Sandy Denny's singing: *who knows where the time goes?*
and it isn't us, still partying on a Sunday afternoon,
slumped on a garden patio beneath a greasy sun,
after a night of pale, crooked lines;
after improvised cocktails of gin and raspberry vodka.

'She died at thirty one', someone says, plucking
an olive from an ashy slick.
'Fell down the stairs.'

And I'm aware I'm wearing grim, glittery rags; yesterday's knickers.
My back to honeysuckled brick, I flick tongue over gums
that taste like a gun in the mouth.

A mobile flashes MUM. No one picks up.
We know how mothers fret over the ticking clocks:
our one-bed flats,
our ovaries.

Instead we fill our plastics up with cider,
and watch wasps as they circle spikes of lavender;
the big sky's cirrus scraps –
a Brimstone butterfly flaps, then settles
on a blackened bone.

My friends, we are so lucky and disgusting,
and will pay for this tomorrow.

The Whale's Tale

But the   scale of
  whale, huge fluke and   hull, the beak an estuary,
  the wealth and store,   the wells of wondrous oils,
    the aquarium, the palatial four-roomed heart, the incense
      of ambergris in a city of entrails, the astonishment.
     Breach, whale – blow! Baptise us in our frail boat
        where the guide tells the miracle – how you
          left the earth, transformed and soared,
            King of the Kingdom of Wet,
             through the heavens of sea,
               to witness us here
               with your 200-year
               old eye. Did the eye
               see Melville, salt-stiff,
               afrizz, as he speared you
             on paper? Does your typewriter
          click-click tell? Leviathan – hold us
                          in your skull's
        library,
             write us in *The Book of Whale*,
                               sing us,
                               sing us
        through ocean,
               and we might not need God.

The Lure
(a ballad)

When you are knackered and cheap food
　　cramps up your guts with pain,
you'll hear the faeries through the glass,
　　beyond the mizzling rain.

They sing: *you deserve more than this –*
　　more than the toil and blame.
Somewhere that's light and glittering.
　　Escape, child, to Elfame.

They lured me barefoot from my bed
　　through night to the wild hill.
I watched it split like a dark skull
　　to show a wondrous hall

with violins and green cupcakes,
　　rubies and perfumed oils,
and cocktails of nightingales' tears,
　　all framed by crystal walls,

and the Erl-Queen in pure gold robes –
　　whose hand I dipped to kiss –
said: *if you look, child, but don't eat,*
　　you can aspire to this.

And so each dusk that Faerie Land
　　called me across the vale.
I'd dance the night with comely men,
　　and leave there drained and pale.

At home I became listless, cold.
　　I would abruptly snap.
I spat their soup out, called them bores,
　　their kindnesses were traps.

They said: *there's beauty here as well*
    in hedge and bloom and day.
There's us... I laughed out loud at that.
    My whole life passed this way.

I knew I deserved more than them,
    More than the hard and plain.
Somewhere that's light and glittering.
    I belonged in Elfame.

Then, one night, thought: what if I ate
    those cakes that they forbid?
What if a morsel means I stay?
    And all illusions fled!

After one crumb the glamour slipped:
    water-rats gnawed in swamps,
the faeries were the grinning dead –
    the hall was a death camp.

It was a blasted, withered place,
    the waste-land where I'd been.
The spell, once broken, broke my heart.
    It smashed like a glass screen.

Beads

(after Attila József)

Beads are fat around your neck,
toad-mouths croaking in the lake.
Droppings glisten,
droppings glisten on its bank.

Round the rose of moon the melt,
round your hips a shining belt.
Knotted rope is
knotted rope is round my throat.

Skirt is drifting round your thighs,
in the bell the bell's tongue sways.
Liquid mirror
holds two pale and splaying trees.

Skirt is drifting round your thighs,
in the bell the bell's tongue cries.
Liquid mirror
thick with mute and stinking leaves.

Babylon

Anyone who falls in love with a system is dangerous
NAOMI KLEIN

It was a city wrought of words and maths,
the king's name stamped on every perfect brick.
Unnatural, with sky-skimming ziggurats;
its lions glazed against some too-blue trick.
A world as seen by waxen, agate eyes
where melons, mint and leak
filled gardens hung in air,
and bulls and barley-stalks were mapped in stars.

It was a city wrought from careful art.
At night fictitious monsters dipped and soared
above the grandeur of the Ishtar Gate –
unnatural, serpent-headed, eagle-clawed.
But even walls no man can penetrate
can't stop the finger's scrawl
when it inscribes the end.
Things fell to whorish slander; slid in sand.

Marmots and jackals now stalk Babylon,
and bombs blast nightly, monstrous, in the squares.
Its new walls are the Green Zone's, manned by guns,
surrounding palaces, hot-tubs and maids.
As heads are severed on a digicam
and chemical loos ooze,
Camp Alpha's marching feet
and helipads disturb the ruins' sleep.

This mess was calculated by the sure,
by all the zealots yearning for blank slates –
though language wrought it too: words like secure
and *freedom*, words you're with or you're against,
contrived, as is this poet's rhyme for war.
Men build such dreams, such gates,
such towers, such agate eyes
that do not flinch when the imperfect die.

Amtssprache

So what would you pay to have your family safe
in that house with the garden and the clean running water –
and you walk in and hold them and kiss their faces?
Your life? Too easy, and nobody's asking.

How about the life of an Afghan child,
a city, the birds in the sky?
Would you turn a blind eye? Would you turn off the news?
Would you run the trains to death camps?

Of course you would. You do.
You do these things.

The Language of Flowers, *or* The Primrose

How many words do you know for shoe?
I know too many too:
the mules and brogues, the ballet-slippers,
platforms, courts, stilettos, wedges,
flip-flops, kitten-heels and mary-janes
and slingbacks and the Ugg.

Once I pressed flowers, so learnt their names –
wrote them by bowed and jaundiced heads –
but then the siren-song of cities cooed from my TV
and I preferred that Esperanto of want and need:
Selfridges, mojitos, latte, weed,
hoodies and nightbus,
Banksy, chorizo,
Noho, lido and burlesque show...

and now the names are lost,
and now I need those blossoms back.
Without the right words, I can't think clearly.
Whoever cared for what's nameless?

I must learn what the Stinking Iris is,
the Harebell, Angel Bonnet, Mother-die;

that *Populus Tremula* means trembling Poplar;
means the Aspen whispering to us
                                    – listen –
through leaves like teeth, chattering with fear.

The City-dweller Laments

The park I must avoid after dark is not enough,
the basil pot in its wrapper is not enough,
the organic cheese is not enough,
the limping pigeon is not enough,
the sunflowers in Sainsburys are not enough.

Lines Written on the Norfolk Broads

We drifted through warm currents. Our hull chugged
past windmills – sails as useless as fishbones –
as Mallards raped, as Egyptian Geese shrugged,
and flocks of plastic bottles caught in reeds.
And then a glimpse of Kingfisher, it zagged –
sky-backed, sun-bellied, rainbowed – out of green.
Illumination in the margin inked
with lapis lazuli. Tiny machine!

And in that blurred half-second how I missed
the bird already – already the pang!
My mouth hadn't the speed to shape the word
'Kingfisher', before it squeaked like the hinge
of a door shutting; pierced the water's chest.
We churn on, through a world too slow, too fast.

The Skulls of Dalston

Of late, overnight, leering graffiti skulls appear
on London's walls – sherbert death-heads,
jack o'lanterns, acme eyeballs pinging
in eye-caves, tombstone teeth in bubblegums.
Mornings also bring mist. A young bloke pisses
on a car, pissed. Nappies bloat in a yard.
Corn-rowed, in tip-to-toe pink, a girl shins
up the building's wall as though it is a tree,
and I'm trying to think this 'edgy' –
white, pushed here by price –
when I pass a boy. Just us on the street.
He drifts through pale air, white air, focused,
jeans low, whole crotch on show, face blacked
by his hood's shadow. Our eyes don't meet.
Why would they? We are not on the same street.

> If I'm a blank, then he's a void,
> if I'm the scum, then he's the dregs,
> if I'm a ghost then he's a shadow,
> if I'm pigeon-shit then he's a crow.

And he's watching for the Love of money crew
the DNA Boys, the Murder Dem Pussies,
and I'm looking at the Arcola theatre, up-
and-coming shows, acting out a play in my head:
rape – the spurt of blood – stairwells –
I am rehearsing a play called Hell.
And I know I don't belong on this street,
and the street belongs to this boy, but on the next
they might kill him, because it is the blue borough,
he cannot tread where the signs and bins are blue,
he cannot cross the turf of the Tap Dem Crew
he cannot cross the turf of the E9 Bang Bang,
he is wearing his slash-proof vest,
he is wearing his shank, just in case,
he is looking out for disrespect in a city
mapped over mine, my phantom city, my city

of the blind: misted cataract, net-curtain.
If I caught his eye in dark, would he slash my neck?
Did the last flowers he bought stay wrapped by the road?
Were they on that front page: FALLEN SOULJA?
Did his friend spurt blood into gutters
as the girls cried: 'Kill him, kill him'
in this forest of walls and skulls?

If I'm the skull then he's the eye-caves,
if I'm teeth then he's the bowels,
if I'm the paper, he's the tabloid ink,
if I'm what he thinks then he's what I think.

So it's best not to look, and he does not see me.
We do not look at each other. It is as though
we are nothing to do with each other.
We are sure we are nothing to do with each other.

Zennor

They crossed the partition –
    first the mermaid at Nunton
        who slithered from netted green;
nightmare silence where catfish skidded,
    whiskered,
        over her chest,
            her shucked eyes.

The cold of the sea is ferocious –
    mottles skin and makes fingers thick red –
        and she wanted to feel the warmth of stones,
    but a boy cast a stone,
caved her skull.

Then the incident in Sheringham:
    it was drawn to the church's spire.
        The beadle yapped: 'Mermaids
    can't come in here!'
Slammed the oak door in her face.

But Zennor was different.
    Beneath dark grey sky,
        smeared with lemon radiance,
    as sanderlings dared the edges of brown waves,
    a mermaid followed a man's voice,

    followed words he sang out:

        Salvation,   *Risen,*
            Love;
        pulled herself out and across and into the town,
    fathom by fathom,
eelgrass and blood under nails –
biting brine-stung lips with concentration.

Though her skin was the colour of seafoam,
and tiny crabs swung in her hair,
Mathew Trewella did not care;
fell in love with this sea-creature –
each sandy inch –

and she'd die out of wet, but was where he belonged,

so he crossed the divide,

waded into his fear, to the waist, to the wincing face,
until he could not feel it,
and she clung to Mathew, arms round his neck,
and kissed his head and throat.

Beloved stranger, he entered a place
of wild and alien light.

The Two Ravens
(a ballad)

As I walked down a street alone,
I heard two ravens make a plan,
one bird unto the other said:
'Which shall we dine on of the dead?'

'Out there upon a dirty track
    way down a down, way down
a woman's spread upon her back,
    in the mud.
her throat cut and her body raped,
for bags of books, a glimpse of face.
    O down, derry derry, if she's bad they're good.

The bird said: 'no one cares she lies
In dust near dogs in smears of flies,
the army's led by fear and oil,
the husband's had his honour spoiled,

'her son's stood in a hood of black
    way down a down, way down
a donkey, ridden, told to crack,
    in the blood.
and other women fear to speak,
which means she'll waste if not for beaks.'
    O down, derry derry, if they're bad she's good.

So low as planes they did swoop down,
to chew on unveiled eyes of brown,
they pecked out clumps of her dark hair
to line their nests when they grew bare.

And many commentators moaned,
    way down a down, way down
but armoured cars drove past the bones.
    and I stood
I watched the ravens feed on war,
and knew I'd watch for evermore.
    O down, derry derry, if she's bad we're good.

The Wood

I

Halfway through my life,
I found myself in a dark wood.
The proper road was lost.
I had been searching for food –
because I had responsibilities,
because no one else would.
I'd thought I'd seen horse mushrooms,
but touched, their flesh bruised yellow,
so I left them there as poison,
and then turned, and all had shifted,
and the breathing forest darkened.
I was in a savage labyrinth,
its columns ancient, buttressed, crusted
with verdigris, the roof
a mosaic of green and turquoise
gargoyled by bitching magpies,
the floor tiled with golden leaves.
It was leaking and trees creaked like closing doors,
and every time a path split, I chose
wronger, I chose darker,
and I had to keep on choosing.
There was only choice or death.

II

Hours later I was snivelling, scratched
by briar, branch-smacked, blackness
came on fast. Stopped by thirst
at the green mouth of a pool,
I drank, slapped my face with the despair of it,
stared dumb on cankered violets,
a hedgehog's guts lit up with maggots,
a rabbit as it ate its own wet child,
beetles fucking – all the shuddering wild.

The moon slid over my head like a stone,
and then a young man trotted out,
fawn-lean, he-she yawned, scratched
her crotch, her arms tattooed with oxlips,
cobwebs, eglantine; eyes green,
her mouth a riddled musk-rose. 'Well –'
'I'm lost,' I said. 'And this is hell.
I have to find my home.'
'*Have?*' she laughed, 'All you have to do is live,'
and she winked and took my hand,
and she fed me bits of mushroom,
and the hurting forest reeled.

III

That night I learned the animal I was,
I chose wronger, I chose darker,
rubbed and sniffed and lapped
at green mouths, puffballs, meat still stiff
with living blood. I loved the ass,
his fair large ears. I felt light
as peaseblossom, a worm-eaten nut.
She smeared me in the uncouth forest,
made me bay, I ripened
in the blackness for her prick.
We drank from waters warped, then, drunk,
I broke a rabbit's neck. I ate.
I carved my name on every tree, and hers,
and let her teach to me
that love deserves the dark house and the whip;
that sex and sweat and flesh and drink and power
are all this body wants –
and he-she showed me beasts lay down with Queens,
girls flew, boys crawled.
I watched her toss dove-chicks to a bright fox;
wings were pulled from butterflies;
Pan sucked his cock.
I licked my fingers.

IV

I woke up emptied – a worm-eaten nut,
a cankered violet, a green mouth,
my wings pulled off.
I was laid flat as if to measure my own grave,
my young man gone, my bowels
aslide with dark.
And though I knew my journey was my story,
when I heard the hounds and horns
and I knew that they had found me,
I must admit I cried with the relief of it –
I let myself be taken back to home.
In their room I found my babies
rocking quiet, kissed their faces,
vowed to them their mother
wouldn't leave the road again,
because I have responsibilities,
I have to feed their mouths.
At night the wood still burns me like green fire,
but I have to keep on choosing.
I am thirty. I am adult. I sing to them:
never harm, nor spell, nor charm,
lulla lulla lullaby.

The Caravan

We were alive that evening, on the north Yorkshire moors,
in a valley of scuffed hills and smouldering gorse.
Pheasants strutted, their feathers as richly patterned
as Moroccan rugs, past the old Roma caravan –
candles, a rose-cushioned bed, etched glass –
that I'd hired to imagine us gipsies
as our bacon and bean stew bubbled,
as you built a fire, moustached, shirt-sleeves rolled.
It kindled and started to lick, and you laughed
in your muddy boots, there in the wild –
or as close as we can now get to the wild –
skinning up a joint with dirty hands, sloshing wine
into beakers, the sky turning heather with night,
the moon a huge cauldron of light,
the chill wind blasting away our mortgage,
emails, bills, TV, our broken washing machine.
Smoke and stars meant my thoughts loosened,
and took off like the owls that circled overhead,
and I knew your hands would later catch in my hair,
hoped the wedding ring on them never seemed a snare –
for if you were a traveller I would not make you settle,
but would have you follow your own weather,
and if you were a hawk I would not have you hooded,
but would watch, dry-mouthed, as you hung above the fields,
and if you were a rabbit I would not want you tame,
but would watch you gambolling through the bracken,
though there is dark meat packed around your ribs,
and the hawk hangs in the skies.